86   87   88   90   91 94 96
95   97   99   02

HISTORY AS EVIDENCE

PREHISTORY

KEITH BRANIGAN
Illustrated by David Salariya and Shirley Willis

Warwick Press

Contents

Editor: Caroline Royds
Designer: Ben White

The publishers wish to thank the following for supplying
photographs for this book: 9 Malcolm Murray; 12 P. J. Reynolds;
15 Somerset Levels Project; 19 The National Museum,
Copenhagen; 20 British Museum; 22 Jean Courtin; 26 Society of
Antiquaries, London; 28 Landesmuseum fur Vorgeschichte, Halle;
30 I. M. Stead; 31 G. Kelsey/Bristol City Museum;
33 R. J. C. Atkinson.

Published 1984 by Warwick Press,
387 Park Avenue South, New York, New York 10016.

First published in Great Britain by
Kingfisher Books Limited 1984.

Printed in Italy by Vallardi Industrie Grafiche, Milan.

Library of Congress Catalog Card No. 84-50696

ISBN 0-531-03745-2

Introduction

Prehistory is the story of the human race in those long and remote periods of time before people began to keep written records. The story began at least two and a half million years ago in East Africa. It lasted there until the European explorations of the continent in the 19th century AD. Europe itself left the prehistoric era during the time of the Roman Empire, while both Egypt and Mesopotamia entered written history soon after 3000 BC.

Until written records were kept there were no recorded calendars either, so prehistory has to be dated by other methods. The most important of these today is radio-carbon dating. Radioactive carbon 14 is absorbed by all living things – plants, animals and people. When they die, the carbon 14 stored within them is slowly lost. It goes at a constant rate: half of it is lost in about 5800 years. By measuring the amount of carbon 14 in the remains of trees, animals or people, we can say when they died; that is we can date them.

Using carbon dating, we can also establish when various human skills were developed. It is clear that they were learned and developed at different times in different places. The time chart at the end of the book will show you how this is true in parts of Europe and the Near East. In the rest of the book we shall look at the evidence archaeologists use to reconstruct life in prehistoric times.

The evidence of prehistory is very different from that of history. It rarely involves great events or great people, but is mostly concerned with the everyday life of ordinary men and women. Unlike written history, prehistory depends on archaeological finds which carry no obvious message for us. The evidence has to be carefully collected and then interpreted. We shall see how evidence selected from ten different sites, widely spread throughout Europe (see the map below), can be used to piece together a picture of how people lived, worked and died in prehistory.

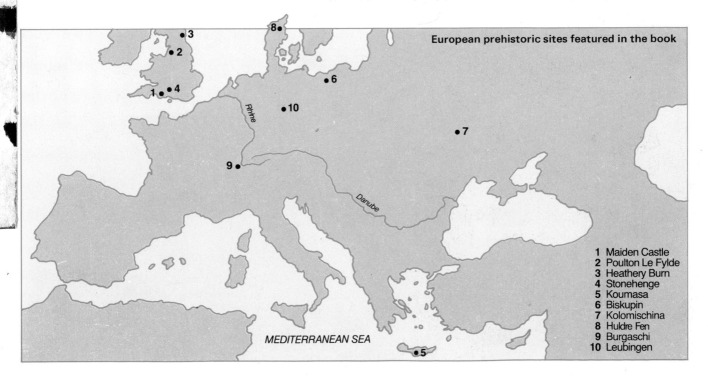

European prehistoric sites featured in the book

Rhine

Danube

MEDITERRANEAN SEA

1 Maiden Castle
2 Poulton Le Fylde
3 Heathery Burn
4 Stonehenge
5 Koumasa
6 Biskupin
7 Kolomischina
8 Huldre Fen
9 Burgaschi
10 Leubingen

Finding Food

Prehistoric people spent much of their time making sure that they had enough food to live on. Until the end of the last Ice Age, about 10,000 BC, they depended entirely on their skills as hunters; later they began to farm and to control the crops and animals they needed.

In trying to understand how early people obtained their food, archaeologists have to bring together a lot of different pieces of evidence. Prehistoric hunters left behind them the weapons they used – axes, spears, and bows and arrows – the hard parts of which, made of flint or other stone, still survive. We also find stone weights from fishing nets, bone fish-hooks, and just occasionally remains of the nets themselves. Although we can easily imagine how such things were used to trap and kill animals, useful clues to the hunting methods of early peoples are also found in the cave paintings and other drawings made by the prehistoric hunters of the last Ice Age. In particular these pictures show how hunters banded together to track down their prey, and they often show the prey itself – deer, horse and bison – so we know what animals were being hunted. But the bones of butchered animals, discovered either at open air camp sites or in the mouths of caves where early hunters lived, are the most reliable evidence for this. Careful study of these bones will even reveal how the carcases were prepared for cooking.

Above: Fishing was important in prehistoric times. Some people used hooks on lines, but many used nets which they cast from their canoes. People who lived near the sea, perhaps for only part of the year, would also collect shells from along the shore and hunt seabirds to supplement and vary their diet. In other seasons these fishermen became inland hunters.

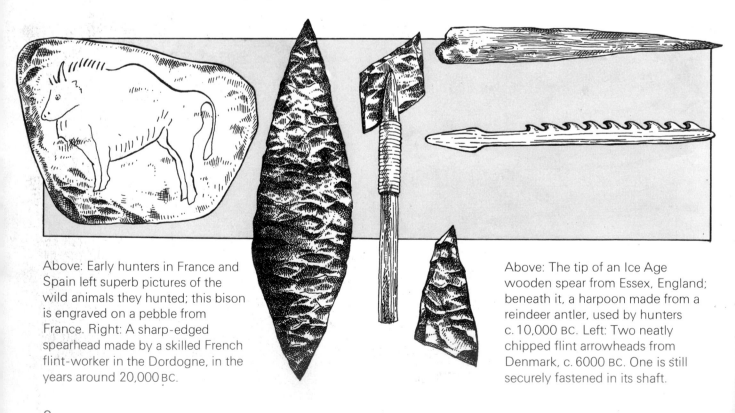

Above: Early hunters in France and Spain left superb pictures of the wild animals they hunted; this bison is engraved on a pebble from France. Right: A sharp-edged spearhead made by a skilled French flint-worker in the Dordogne, in the years around 20,000 BC.

Above: The tip of an Ice Age wooden spear from Essex, England; beneath it, a harpoon made from a reindeer antler, used by hunters c. 10,000 BC. Left: Two neatly chipped flint arrowheads from Denmark, c. 6000 BC. One is still securely fastened in its shaft.

Whereas the hunters were forced to move around searching out and following their prey, most farmers lived permanently in one place. Their houses and surroundings can be recognized as farms because of certain unusual buildings. As well as a house, a farmer might need a barn or granary, a threshing floor or an animal pen. Archaeologists are able to recognize these from the remains they find in their excavations.

Around the farm it may still be possible to trace the boundaries of prehistoric fields. These often survive as low banks of stones cleared from the fields or as lines of post-holes which once held the upright supports for wooden fences. Within these fields, buried deep beneath the modern ground level, there may still be grooves left in the soil by the ancient plow which oxen dragged across the field. The iron tips of the plow (or plow-shares) are sometimes found, and even wooden plows have occasionally survived for thousands of years. So have other tools which tell us something about prehistoric farming techniques – wooden digging sticks weighted with a perforated stone, wooden hoes, and sickles with wood or bone handles and flint teeth.

The crops cut with these sickles have mostly perished long ago, but sometimes grain was charred by fire and preserved, so archaeologists can identify it as wheat, barley or oats. The careful study of preserved bones can tell us not only which animals were domesticated in prehistoric times, but even whether sheep were kept mainly for wool or meat.

Above: The coming of farming led to important changes in the landscape. To make fields and grow crops, farmers had to cut down many acres of trees. The wood was used to build houses, barns and pens for animals. The animals themselves had to be tamed or "domesticated" from wild species of sheep and cattle. At first farming may have been just as hard work as hunting.

Right: These plow marks of about 1500 BC were preserved beneath sand in Cornwall, England. Below: A sickle with flint teeth, a wooden hoe, and carbonized grain.

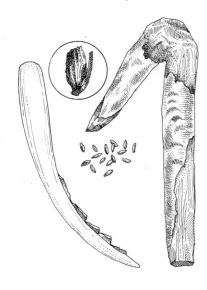

Finding Food

AN ELK HUNT

Here we see the end of an elk hunt which took place at Poulton-le-Fylde, England, around 9000 BC. A vivid reconstruction of the event is possible because archaeologists recovered the complete skeleton of the animal, together with bone harpoon heads, in the silted-up bed of a prehistoric pool. Tree-pollen showed that the pond was surrounded by birch trees, and the condition of the elk's antlers indicated it had died in winter. Careful study of the skeleton suggested the animal was from 4 to 6 years old, and had been attacked and wounded over a period of perhaps nine or ten days. Some of the wounds were sharp gashes made by flint-tipped arrows, others were made by heavier weapons – probably axes – and some were made by bone "harpoon" heads, two of which were found with the skeleton. Using all this information, we can imagine the dramatic scene that winter 11,000 years ago.

A group of four or five hunters has been pursuing a strong male elk for over a week. They have wounded it in the hind legs and, as the wounds have swollen over the days, the animal has slowed down. Now the hunters move in for the kill. First they strike the elk with flint-tipped arrows from their wooden bows, then manage to close in and inflict several blows with axes and clubs. The prey is almost within their grasp. Using its last reserves of strength, the animal makes a desperate attempt to escape across the ice of the nearby pond. But the ice is too thin for its weight. It gives way and the struggling animal sinks beneath the surface. The hunters can only watch in frustration and disbelief as their prey disappears from view. Now they will probably go hungry for the next few days until they find and track another animal.

10

Finding Food

The coming of farming led to the widespread appearance of permanent farmsteads and villages throughout Europe. Because farmers can control their animals, and because they need to till, sow and reap their fields, they will lead a more settled existence than hunters. But they may still hunt animals, catch fish and gather wild fruits to ensure the family has enough food.

At Burgaschi in northern Switzerland, archaeologists have uncovered the remains of a typical early farming settlement. Like many of its kind in Switzerland, it was built on the marshy ground at the edge of a lake. Over three thousand wooden piles or stakes cut from the nearby forest were driven into the soft ground to make a firm base on which to build the settlement. An area 160 feet long and 30 feet wide was surrounded by a wooden palisade or fence, and through three entrances ran trackways made of more logs laid horizontally on the ground. These tracks served the three buildings erected inside the enclosure. Two were probably houses, perhaps occupied by ten or a dozen people each. The low walls were of wooden boards and wickerwork, and the roofs were thatched with grass or reeds. The third building was simply a covered working area.

Above: The rugged Soay sheep of today are direct descendants of sheep that were bred by prehistoric farmers.

Right: This reconstruction of the farming settlement at Burgaschi is based on well-preserved evidence. Part of the wooden palisade and the trackways had survived because of the damp conditions on the site. Similarly, both the upright posts and fragments of wattle and boarding from the walls of the houses were preserved. No trace of roofing material was found, but the strength of the roof supports and the availability of materials in the area suggest reed or grass thatch. The cultivation of crops was proved by the discovery of sickles and a hoe, as well as actual grains of wheat and barley. The small hut to the right, which had no walls, was probably a covered working area. In spite of their farming skills, the people of Burgaschi still relied on hunting for much of their meat. They caught wild animals in the nearby forest, and probably ate the meat of deer, boar and wild cattle much more often than that of the pigs and sheep they kept.

Clues to the lives of the farmers at Burgaschi come both from the surroundings of the settlement, and from the preserved remains found within it. Right beside the enclosure was a broad, flat strip of fertile land suitable for growing crops. Beyond it stretched mixed forest of oak, ash and alder trees. On the other side of the settlement was the lake, a rich source of fish and water birds. The flint arrowheads and bone harpoons found in the settlement were probably used for hunting them.

Sickles and a hoe were found as evidence that the people of Burgaschi grew crops on the land outside the palisade. From preserved grains of emmer wheat and barley we know what kinds of grain were grown. Remains of flax show that these people would have been able to produce linen, and the sheep they reared and the deer they killed also provided wool and skins for clothing. In the forest beyond the fields they kept pigs and, more important, hunted deer, boar and wild cattle. Since they also made their own pottery and tools of bone, flint and wood, the people of Burgaschi must have led very busy lives for most of the year. Men, women and chidren must all have played a part in providing the settlement with everything it needed.

Above: A woman grinding grain into flour on a flat millstone called a quern. She rubs the grain back and forth between the large stone and a smaller one held in her hands. The raw grain will be stored in one of the clay pots by her side, and the flour will be put in the other.

Making Things

One of the skills which sets humans apart from other animals is the ability to make things – tools, weapons, clothing, containers – and when those things are broken, to make them again and again. Even the earliest men and women were capable of making simple tools.

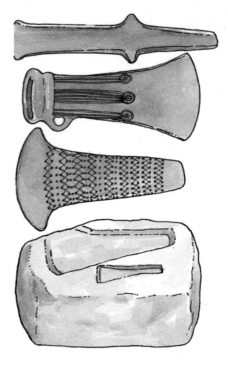

The first stone axes were very simple, but as time passed people learned how to make more efficient ones. By about 300,000 BC, finely shaped hand-axes were in use throughout Europe. Long before the end of the Ice Age, about 10,000 BC, flint-workers were producing tool kits which included awls, knives and scrapers, as well as arrowheads and spearheads. By 4000 BC, the demand for flint tools and weapons was such that there were probably specialist flint-workers who dug elaborate mines into the chalk where the best flint was to be found. Filled-in mine shafts and debris from flint working can still be seen at Spienne in Belgium and Grimes Graves in England.

Gradually, stone tools were replaced by metal ones. By 3000 BC, tools and other objects made of copper were common in the lands around the Mediterranean, and by 2000 BC they were being produced throughout Europe. Apart from the thousands of objects which survive, we have the remains of casting molds, furnaces and working tools as evidence of how the bronzesmiths plied their craft. Analysis of their products also tells us a great deal about their skills.

Above: Evidence for the craft of the bronze-smith usually takes the form of tools and moulds like these. The chisel, socketed axe and flat axe would all have been useful for the prehistoric carpenter. Axes were cast in the mould first, and later hammered into their final shape.

Left: Four particularly common tools used by Bronze Age carpenters. Such tools are the best surviving pieces of evidence we have for the ancient craft of carpentry. On the far left is a broad chisel for smoothing the surface of cut planks. Next to it is a single ax which could be used for trimming small branches off a felled tree. The curious implement second left is an ax-adz, a particularly useful tool for trimming and shaping the rough-cut timber. Finally we have a small saw suitable for cutting through smaller pieces of timber. The carpenter made his own tool handles (which have not normally survived) but depended on the bronzesmith for his tools. Since there was no money the craftsmen must have exchanged goods.

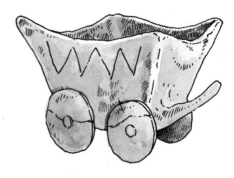

Above: This clay model of a wagon from Hungary dates from about 2000 BC. The zigzag lines on the side may represent ropes used to tie down loads. A few wooden wagon wheels have survived for thousands of years – usually in very wet or very dry conditions – but we rely on models like this one to give us some idea of the vehicles on which they were mounted.

Just as flint tools were replaced by bronze ones, so in time bronze was largely replaced by iron. After about 1000 BC, iron tools and weapons became increasingly common in the east Mediterranean, and by 500 BC they were used all over Europe. Although iron was more difficult to work than bronze, it made more durable tools, and iron ores were more widely spread. For these reasons we find evidence of iron working, mainly in the form of waste material (slag) and furnaces, on many late prehistoric sites. The introduction first of bronze and then of iron tools led to important developments in other crafts, particularly carpentry. At the same time as we begin to find bronzesmiths making saws, chisels, gouges, adzes and other woodworking tools, we also find models of tables and chairs, seagoing ships and wheeled wagons. Under the right conditions, some of these things have survived until the present day – chairs from Egypt, tables from the tombs of Jericho, boats from England and wagon wheels from the Netherlands.

Prehistoric carpenters also made looms for weaving cloth, and frequent evidence for spinning and weaving is provided by clay spindle whorls (or weights) and loom weights. Although the cloth itself is rarely preserved, models and figurines help us to imagine what prehistoric clothes were like. Spinning and weaving were probably family crafts, practiced by every household in a prehistoric village. In the same way, people made their own bone combs and needles, their baskets, their leather belts and caps, and in most cases their own pottery. They also had to build their own homes.

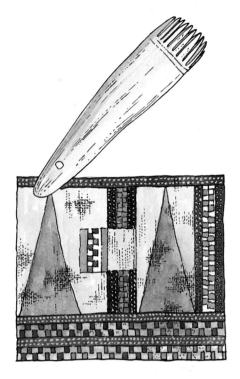

Above: This piece of linen textile was preserved in damp conditions in a Neolithic village in Switzerland. The bone comb may have been for combing wool. Because cloth rarely survives, spindle whorls and loom-weights are more common evidence of spinning and weaving.

Right: Some of the rare examples of wood to have survived from prehistoric times, the pieces seen here are about 3000 years old. These planks, found preserved in peat in England, reveal that Bronze Age carpenters were highly skilled craftsmen. Working with nothing more elaborate than the tools seen on the opposite page, they were able to fell large trees and cut them into regular planks like these. The planks were used in buildings which were put together without any nails. As you can see, the planks had square holes neatly cut through them to allow other timbers to be jointed with them. Similar techniques were used in manufacturing furniture and boats as well as looms for weavers.

Making Things

Biskupin in Poland is an exceptional prehistoric site. In trying to understand the skills of the ancient carpenters, we usually have to depend on a selection of the tools they used, rare clay models of furniture and vehicles, and the ground plan of timber houses traced out by the holes in which the wooden posts once stood. But at Biskupin waterlogged conditions have preserved the timber buildings of this remarkable township of about 600 BC.

The settlement was built on an island and strongly defended by a continuous palisade fronted by a timber breakwater. Within the safety of the defenses lived about 600 people, in rows of tidy little terrace houses. The houses were built on either side of timber-paved streets, which were all linked together by a ring-road which ran around the town. In some of the houses lived metalworkers who produced tools, weapons and trinkets for the rest of the population. In other houses there were spinners and weavers, and in others those who worked in bone and horn. The rest of the people were probably farmers.

The building of the settlement and its defenses was a major task which required a great deal of hard work as well as skilled carpentry. Over 200,000 cubic feet of timber – oak and pine – had to be felled, trimmed, brought to the site and then cut to size. The construction work was probably carried out by skilled craftsmen using iron axes, adzes, chisels and gouges. First they laid out the lines of defenses, streets and houses. Then they probably built the elaborate rampart – a series of wooden boxes filled with earth. A timber gateway with a guard tower above was placed at the end of the 400-feet-long long causeway.

The buildings were constructed in long rows, with up to ten houses under one thatched roof. The walls were of logs, laid horizontally one above the other and held by uprights. As well as a living room, each house had a porch area. Doors were of wattle, and stone hearths were set in the center of the wooden floor. Inevitably, with naked fires in wooden buildings, there were accidents. Here houses are being repaired after they have been damaged by fire.

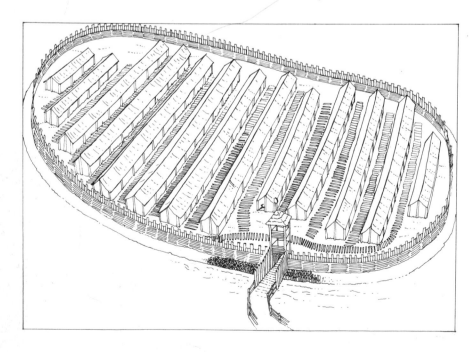

Making Things

Spinning wool and weaving cloth are crafts which have been practiced since well before 4000 BC. The earliest evidence for them is the appearance of whorls which acted as weights on the spindles, and of larger and heavier weights for use on looms. Throughout prehistory the main evidence we have for making cloth remains these simple weights, although bone weaving tablets and woolcombs are sometimes found, and very rarely fragments of wooden frames which may have come from looms.

For the cloth itself, and the garments made from it, we have to rely mainly on figurines and small fragments of preserved material. But there is one notable exception: in the peat bogs of Denmark, people buried in the period 1200–400 BC have been found, still fully clothed, the cloth and their bodies preserved by the waterlogged peat. From these unique finds we can learn much about cloth making and changing fashions in prehistoric Denmark. Around 1200 BC, Danish men wore oval cloaks over simple wraps which covered either the body and the upper legs, or else the legs alone. On their heads they wore round caps, sewn in simple pieces from rough woolen cloth rather like a modern towel. The women had more attractive and elaborate clothes. They too wore bonnets, or plaited hair nets, but their jackets had elbow-length sleeves and were sometimes embroidered. In addition to a full length skirt suitable for cold, northern winters, they also wore short, loose string skirts.

Above: An Iron Age drawing of a figure in a decorated dress spinning with a spindle and whorl. The whorl, seen near the end of the yarn, was a clay or stone weight fixed on the spindle. Many of these have been found, and are our most common pieces of evidence for prehistoric spinning.

Right: This reconstruction of a prehistoric loom is based partly on pictures drawn on pottery and partly on the evidence found in a house excavated in the village of Ginderup. On the floor of the hut, between two post-holes was a pile of clay loomweights. These would have been tied onto the ends of the vertical threads. The woman is using a bone comb, of a type commonly found in the Iron Age, to comb the woolen threads. All of the woolen clothes found in the Danish bogs could have been woven on a loom such as this. The remains of such looms rarely survive, but a fragment of one has been found inside a pot in the bog of Dejbjerg. Upright looms of this sort were a big improvement on the first horizontal looms invented by prehistoric people which could only make a piece of material as long as the loom itself.

Right: These two sets of women's clothes were found close to one another in Huldre Fen, Jutland. The tartan skirt and cape were actually found on the preserved body of a woman. The tartan pattern was created by using wool of two contrasting shades of brown – one a light golden color, the other much darker. The way in which the material was slightly gathered at one side during weaving shows that this piece of material was woven specifically for a skirt. The dress on the far right is rather like an open-ended sack, about 5 feet long. The turned-over top drapes over the upper arms or can be turned up as a hood.

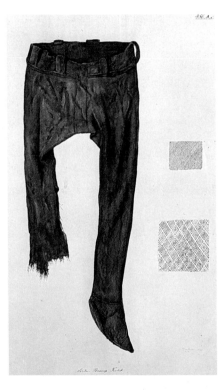

Above: This pair of men's pants was found at Thorsbjerg in Denmark and belongs to the end of the prehistoric period. They were part of a collection of many objects which had apparently been deposited at a sacred spot as an offering. Caesar, the Roman general, tells us that the people of this region offered booty to their war god in this way.

Although fashion changed slowly in prehistory, by about 400 BC Danish men and women wore clothes which were quite different in design from those just described. From Huldre Fen in Jutland come two sets of women's clothes. One includes a lambskin cape and a tartan skirt fastened with a leather strap, and the other is a long tubular dress. This apparently shapeless garment could be gathered at the waist with a girdle, and turned over at the top to form a hood. It was very similar in design to the dresses being worn at the same time almost 1200 miles away in Greece.

Finds from other European sites reveal that the women often bound their hair into either a ponytail or two pigtails, and wore delicate, net-like bonnets. Rather less survives of the clothes worn by men, although it seems that deerskin capes and leather sandals were common. In the 1st century AD, the Roman writer Tacitus tells us that the Germans wore a garment that fitted closely on every limb, and this may well be that shown on a Danish cauldron found at Gundestrup, where the warriors wear tight-fitting tunics with long sleeves and knee-length pants.

Making Things

One of the most important crafts in later prehistory was metalworking, whether in bronze or iron. The metalworker forged the weapons with which people defended themselves in war, and the ornaments and jewelry they wore in peace. Most important of all, he made the wide variety of tools on which other craftsmen depended. The home of a bronzesmith of about 700 BC was discovered in a cave at Heathery Burn in northern England. Among the contents of the cave were the tools and materials of the smith's trade, some of the things he made, and other belongings which tell us something about the way he and his family lived.

The occupied parts of the cave were between 10 and 30 feet wide and about 10 feet high, with a natural floor of sand and gravel. A small stream ran through part of the cave. Smithing probably took place near the entrance, where the light was better and the smoke from the working hearth would clear away most quickly. We can imagine the scene as the smith set to work.

First the fire in the working hearth had to be raised to a high temperature – about 1800°F – with a pair of bellows. Once this was achieved, a crucible containing some scrap metal – bits of broken swords, axes and knives – and perhaps a piece of an ingot of new copper, was placed in position. While the metal melted, the smith bound his two-piece molds together and made sure they were firmly bedded down and level in the sand on the floor of the cave. Then the crucible was carefully lifted from the fire with a pair of tongs and the molten metal poured into the molds. The metal hardened quickly and, once it had cooled, the smith broke the mold into its two halves and took out the socketed ax he had cast. For the moment he laid it on one side. Later, when he had made seven or eight such axes, he would trim unwanted metal off the edges and harden the cutting edge by hammering it. Today he was making axes, tomorrow he would perhaps make spearheads, and the day after that rings and pins. He could make something for everyone, be it weapons, tools or jewelry. When he had sufficient stock to make the journey worthwhile, he would set off to the nearby farms and villages to trade his goods for other things he needed.

While the smith sweated away over the fire and anvil, the other members of the family were also busy. They kept sheep and perhaps a few cattle, and these needed tending. The wool from the sheep had to be spun on weighted spindles. Hides from slaughtered cattle and from wild animals such as deer and fox had to be stripped and cleaned. They kept some of these for their own use, but others could be profitably traded. In this way the family acquired corn, pottery, and shale and amber jewelry.

Above: These objects all betray the workshop of a bronzesmith in the cave at Heathery Burn. At the top is a mold for casting a looped and socketed ax; beneath it the "jets" of waste bronze from casting, and below this one of the cast axes. At the bottom are two socketed tools, and at the left are a pair of bronze tongs used by the smith.

Living Together

Just as people had to learn how to produce food and make things, so they had to learn how to live together, not just in a family but in communities of several hundred people. Working out how our prehistoric ancestors organized themselves, and allowed themselves to be organized, is a fascinating and difficult task for the archaeological detective.

In certain parts of the world, there are still groups of people who live in much the same way as prehistoric societies, without the benefits of modern technology, medicine or written laws. The study of these groups, "anthropology", suggests ways in which prehistoric peoples may have organized themselves, but firm evidence is difficult to find and interpret.

The plans of houses and settlements provide us with useful clues. Throughout prehistory by far the most common type of house was only large enough to accommodate a "nuclear" family – that is parents and their children. This, then, was probably the basic social unit in which most people lived. But sometimes, as in eastern Europe around 4000 BC, we find long houses with two or three domestic hearths which suggest that "extended" families – parents, children and grandchildren – all lived under one roof. Where all the houses in a settlement are of roughly the same size and shape, as in the village of Biskupin in Poland, we think of a community of equals. But a larger, better furnished house in a prominent position may have been the home of a chieftain.

Above: This gruesome scene was found in a rock tomb at Roaix in southern France. The bodies of men were piled on one another, and the flint heads of arrows were found still stuck in some of the bodies. Hastily buried, it is thought that these were the victims of a prehistoric battle in about 2500 BC. Such episodes were probably not uncommon.

Left: The tomb at Stoney Littelton in England is one of the thousands of prehistoric tombs which still survive above ground in Europe, their graves and burial chambers protected by the round or long barrows of earth and stone which cover them. Many of them were probably the burial places of local chieftains and their families, but it must have taken the efforts of a larger community to build the Stoney Littelton tomb in about 3000 BC. It is about 100 feet long, half as wide, and 10 feet high. Its walls and burial chambers are built of blocks of limestone. All of this effort provided just seven burial chambers. Although each may have contained two or three burials, there were probably only 20 to 25 people buried here over 400–500 years.

Above: This plan of a village in the Ukraine around 3000 BC suggests a certain amount of organization, with either communal halls or a chieftain's huts at its center. The houses in the village are like that shown on the right, with between two and four identical rooms, each with oven, platform and table under one roof. They may have been occupied by an extended family – parents, children and grandchildren. The village was supplied with pottery (above right) by specialist potters.

Just as the homes of chieftains stand out from the homes of others, so may their tombs. Some of these were clearly built as much to impress the living as to house the dead: they required large amounts of manpower to build them, yet the number of people buried within is very small. Further evidence of the role or status of the dead may come from the personal belongings buried with them. Elaborate regalia made of precious metals, and luxuries, perhaps imported from distant lands, are normally reserved for chieftains. But craftsmen were also important members of society, and they were sometimes buried with the tools of their trade or some typical product of their craft. In the same way, men buried with hunting equipment or weapons may have been renowned for their skills as hunters or warriors.

Warfare and combat were certainly a part of prehistoric life, and they are often clearly revealed in cemeteries and settlements. Apart from the weapons found in graves and homes alike, the study of prehistoric skeletons often reveals the wounds of war. Moreover the size and the complexity of the defenses built around settlements indicate how much effort people put into defending themselves.

Living Together

Night falls on the village of Kolomischina in the Ukraine. Built by farmers around 3000 BC, it stood on a spur overlooking a river, surrounded by the fields in which its people worked. The village comprised about twenty large houses and about a dozen smaller huts, arranged in a roughly circular plan. At the center of the open space between the houses stood two more large huts, including the largest one in the village. In order to understand how the community was organized we must examine the houses and their contents.

The houses were all built in the same manner, with wattle and daub walls erected on a timber frame. The floors were made of logs covered with clay, and in each room of the house there was an oven, table and platform. Each house, measuring 30 to 40 feet long, had two or three such rooms. These two or three rooms, each equipped for cooking and serving food, under one roof suggest that the houses were occupied by an extended family. A "household" at Kolomischina might number as many as eighteen people.

With about twenty such houses, the population of the village may have been between two and three hundred people. Such a large number of people living together in one place would have to have some kind of leadership. There may have been some sort of village council which could meet in the large buildings at the center of the village. But it is possible that the village had a chief, and that the buildings in the middle belonged to him. In any event, the central area was probably used for communal meetings, festivals and ceremonies.

Some members of the village may have been important not because they were leaders but because they were craftsmen. One house was exceptional in having three ovens in one room; it may have been the home of a potter making the brightly painted vessels used by the villagers. The making of simple copper tools and trinkets – things like fish hooks, rings and beads –

may have been the work of one man too. But every family practiced household crafts such as spinning and carving bone and antler tools. For the most part each family was self-sufficient.

We do not know whether each family had its own fields or whether the surrounding fields were farmed communally. Wheat and barley were grown; the villagers kept

sheep in the pastures, while cattle and pigs were perhaps grazed nearer the river. Certainly the village produced almost everything it needed – only copper and a few larger copper tools (axes and picks) had to be traded from lands far to the west. The inhabitants of Kolomischina seem to have learned how to live together – a peaceful if somewhat isolated existence.

Living Together

People have fought and killed each other since human life began. As they learned new skills such as flint-working and making metal, so they used their new knowledge to make better weapons. Throughout prehistory as well as history, there has been an "arms race" with people seeking to produce better weapons than their neighbors. Improvements in offensive weapons are followed by improvements in defensive armor. As people learned to live together in ever larger communities, so they improved the way they organized themselves for war and defended their towns and villages from attack.

By the end of the 1st century BC, highly defended settlements, which we call hillforts, had become commonplace in western Europe. Maiden Castle in England is a superb example of a hillfort, and excavations there have given us clues as to how it was attacked and captured. It was a formidable target, defended by two (and in places three) complete circuits of high ramparts and deep ditches. Attackers who managed to clamber over the first rampart and slither to the bottom of the ditch inside it were then faced with a steep slope over 80 feet high. If the attackers chose instead to attack the gateways more surprises awaited them. They had to find their way, under fire, through an elaborate maze of ditches and banks and, if they succeeded, were faced with strong timber gates and a horde of hostile defenders on the ramparts above. The defenders were armed with slings, spears and swords, so that they could harass attackers at every step of the way. Given such defenses Maiden Castle must have seemed impregnable.

Above: Dramatic evidence of the defence of the hillfort at Maiden Castle. The skeleton of one defender has an iron bolt in its spine fired from an attacker's powerful catapult. Among other remains, skulls have been found split in two by iron swords.

Left: A pile of slingstones found at Maiden Castle. Heaps of these stones were kept at key points round the ramparts as ammunition dumps. With a sling, the defenders of the fort could reach attackers beyond the farthest ramparts.

In fact, the stronghold was taken and its defenders massacred in the space of a few hours. Julius Caesar described how the Iron Age tribes in France attacked hillforts:

> "They surround the whole circuit of the walls with a large number of men and shower it with stones from all sides, so that the defenses are denuded of men. Then they ... set fire to the gates and undermine the walls."

This is roughly what seems to have happened at Maiden Castle. While the defenders hurled slingstones at them, the attackers fired iron bolts over the ramparts from portable catapults. Then they surged against the east gate and burned it down. Once inside, they cut down the defenders, whose bodies were later buried outside the gateway. Who were the attackers and when did they attack? The use of catapults betrays the presence of the Roman army, and a Roman historian, Suetonius, tells us that the Romans were fighting in this area in AD 43.

Below: The Roman attack on Maiden Castle is recreated in the picture below. The barrage of deadly iron bolts from the Roman catapults set up beyond the ramparts has just finished. Inside the fort, some of the defenders lie mortally wounded, while the rest return to the top of the ramparts where they will soon be needed. The Romans, meanwhile, have set fire to the huts outside the gateway and under cover of the smoke are advancing on the gates of the fort. Once their "tortoise" has broken through or fired the gates, the rest of the legion will burst into the fort and slaughter its defenders – men and women alike will be put to the sword.

Living Together

The wealthy and powerful members of any society usually surround themselves with luxuries which the majority of the people cannot afford. They live in larger houses, have more personal property, and when they die they have an elaborate funeral and an imposing tombstone. So it was in prehistory, and we can sometimes recognize prehistoric chieftains by their impressive tombs and luxurious grave goods.

In central Europe in the period around 2000–1500 BC, many people lived in villages and were buried in communal cemeteries. Their graves were simply pits dug in the ground and their grave goods would perhaps include simple bronze or bone jewelry, and a bronze dagger or ax. Such burials are very different from the tomb uncovered at Leubingen in East Germany where an impressive barrow covers a burial accompanied by a wealth of stone, bronze and gold objects. There are good reasons for calling this a chieftain burial. The barrow was over 100 feet across and 25 feet high. Under a cairn or pyramid of stones at its center was a skillfully constructed wooden burial chamber. The skeleton of an elderly man lay inside; placed over it was that of a younger person, perhaps a woman. Around them was a neatly laid out selection of grave goods. Great effort, skill and care had obviously been lavished on this burial.

Below: A reconstruction of the timber burial chamber found at Leubingen in East Germany. The chamber lay at the center of a stone cairn. Incredibly the timberwork had been preserved and was found when the barrow was excavated in 1877. The chamber, which was shaped like a tent, had obviously been built by a skilled carpenter. The seven pairs of sloping beams, for example, were each carefully jointed into the ridge beam. Over the beams, planks were placed and these were then covered with thatch. Inside, the grave goods were carefully laid out in little groups around the two skeletons. The body laid across the chieftain's waist is thought to be that of a woman.

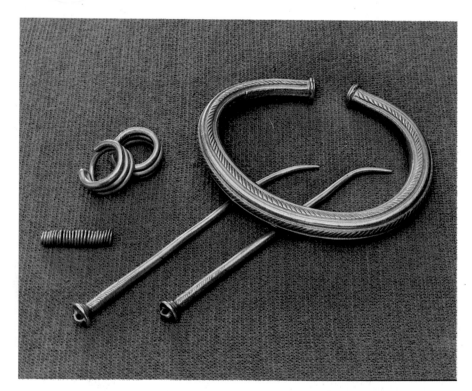

Above: Of all the grave goods at Leubingen, the most impressive were the gold pieces of jewelry. The richly decorated armlet and coiled earrings were purely decorative, but the two long pins were used to fix the man's cloak to his tunic. The other object is a bead.

By looking more closely at the grave goods so carefully arranged about the bodies, we can perhaps understand their special significance. To one side of the man's head lay two long gold cloak pins, two gold earrings, and a superbly decorated gold armlet. The precious metal and the high craftsmanship both imply that their owner was a wealthy man, and these objects were symbols of that wealth. By his legs lay three bronze daggers and a halberd – a weapon a bit like a dagger but fixed on a shaft like an ax. So many weapons might well suggest that the man was honored as a warrior. More difficult to understand, perhaps, are the bronze tools found nearby – three chisels and two axes – for it seems unlikely that the man was also renowned as a carpenter. But as a chieftain he may well have been responsible for arranging the supply of such tools to the village craftsmen, and their presence in the grave may symbolize that power. At his feet lay a whetstone, for sharpening the edges of weapons, and a stone ax. Similar objects have been found in other important prehistoric burials, and they may have been common items of a chief's regalia. All this evidence, taken together, suggests that the man buried at Leubingen was indeed a chieftain who had been given a ceremonial burial.

Above: This picture of the Leubingen chieftain is based on the evidence found and recorded in the tomb, and on evidence found on other sites of the same period in northern Europe. The short tunic is similar to examples found in the Danish bog burials of this time. We know that cloaks were often part of the burials, and we can be sure that there was one at Leubingen because two long gold cloak pins were found in the tomb. His daggers were probably worn at the waist tucked into a leather belt, while the ax head and halberd may well have been carried as symbols of his chieftain's authority. The gold armlet, rings and bead, were certainly status symbols. A man buried with such care and with such a display of wealth was probably more important than a village chieftain; he may well have been the chief of a small tribe.

Religion

To prehistoric peoples, nature was mysterious, all powerful and uncontrollable. But their survival depended on it. It is not surprising, therefore, that they believed in supernatural powers and the importance of appeasing them through sacrifice and worship.

Understanding the religion of prehistoric peoples is particularly difficult for two reasons: the first problem is to identify those things which were used in ritual, the second to understand the beliefs and ideas behind the ritual. A structure can be identified as a temple or shrine by its unusual plan, or by its unusual contents. There may also be traces of ceremonies around it – the remains of large fires or, perhaps, pits full of the bones of sacrificed animals. These things are evidence of a society's communal religion.

The private religion of individuals may be represented by figurines and protective amulets. Some figurines are perhaps no more than toys, but others which show people worshiping or carrying symbols, such as a sun sign or a star, were probably religious objects. But what the figurines, temples and other ritual objects meant in terms of religious belief is something we can never know. We can only use our imagination, and knowledge of modern primitive religions, to make a few guesses.

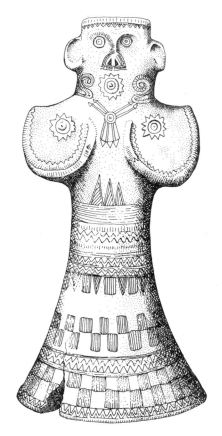

Above: This figurine from Yugoslavia wears an elaborately decorated dress, as well as an impressive necklace and breast ornaments. Figurines, particularly of women, are among the commonest ritual objects found on prehistoric sites. Often the women's bodies are naked, with emphasized breasts, and may have been images of the goddess of fertility.

Left: An Iron Age man buried with his chariot. In prehistoric times many bodies were buried, like this one, with their most important belongings. Other people, with different beliefs about the afterlife, cremated their dead, and then buried the ashes in an urn. Some societies simply left their dead exposed to scavengers and decay.

Above: A group of grave goods from a burial in Scotland. It includes a drinking cup, eight arrowheads and a wrist guard belonging to an archer. This tells us what the dead man did when he was alive, as well as what people thought he should take with him into the afterlife.

When we consider that part of religion which is concerned with death and an afterlife, we can at least identify ritual sites and objects with confidence. A grave or tomb is, by definition, a place of funerary ritual, so everything found there must have been selected to play a part in that ritual. Some things found in graves may have been specially made as funerary objects. We can identify these because they are unsuitable for everyday use and rarely turn up in the houses of the living. The possessions of the dead were also buried with them, and can tell us something of a person's wealth and status in life, and even about his or her occupation.

Other grave goods give us some idea of what people thought about life after death. Supplies of food and new tools or weapons were probably meant to equip the dead for the next world. Old and worn personal belongings have been found, left not as supplies but rather to avoid the risk of haunting by the dead spirit. Fear of the dead, or of their spirits, may also be reflected in the way the body has been treated and the way the tomb has been closed. There is some evidence that further rituals took place at tombs long after the funeral. This suggests that people believed the dead could intercede with the gods on behalf of the living, and so continued to appeal to them for help. Life and death, then as now, were closely intertwined.

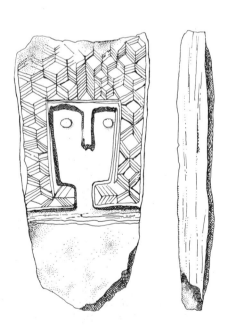

Above: This schematic face, carved on an upright stone slab known as a statue-menhir, is from Provence in France. It was probably a religious symbol.

Above: These curious carvings of feet were pecked into the surface of a stone grave slab in Somerset. Early people spent many hours carving religious symbols onto pieces of stone and rock faces, and these feet carvings probably had a religious significance.

31

Religion

Between 3000 and 1500 BC, there were over one thousand places in Britain alone which were probably used for important communal ritual. Stonehenge in Wiltshire is certainly the most famous of these.

The first sacred works at Stonehenge were built about 2500 BC. A circular area was enclosed by a bank and outer ditch. At the entrance stood two upright stones, and about 100 feet outside stood a third large stone, now known as the Heel Stone. About 2000 BC, the first stone circles were erected. Two concentric rings of 38 upright stones were placed inside the enclosure. At the same time an avenue was laid out as an approach to the monument. Significant as the stone circles are, the most important feature of this new temple was the source of the stones. They were "bluestones", mainly dolerite, from the Prescelly Mountains of Wales. Altogether 82 of these stones, weighing up to 4 tons each, were hauled and carried by raft along a route over 200 miles long.

Greater efforts were still to come. Sometime around 1500 BC, nearly eighty more stones were hauled to the site. These sarsen stones were brought from only twenty miles away, but they averaged 26 tons each! Each was dressed and shaped, and then the famous continuous stone circle was erected. At its center were raised the five huge trilithons, each made of two upright stones and a lintel. Stonehenge was now a unique monument.

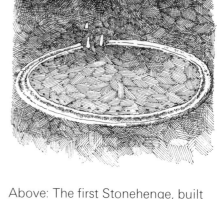

Above: The first Stonehenge, built about 2500 BC, was a relatively simple monument. Yet the digging of the ditch with antler picks and shovels made from the shoulder blades of oxen was a major task. So was the transport and erection of the Heel Stone, which weighs over 20 tons.

The final temple at Stonehenge represents both a prolonged effort by thousands of workers, and some ingenious engineering. The huge sarsen stones had to be back-achingly hauled on hundreds of rollers for over 20 miles and then erected. Careful study of the holes in which the stones stand suggests how they were put upright (right). An oblong hole was dug, with a sloping ramp on one side and a row of wooden posts on the other (A). The stone was rolled to the edge and then levered until it slid in (B). It was then pulled and levered upright (C). The lintel stones, weighing a mere 7 tons each, were probably lifted on a cradle (D). This was built up timber by timber (E), until the lintel could be levered into its position atop the upright (F).

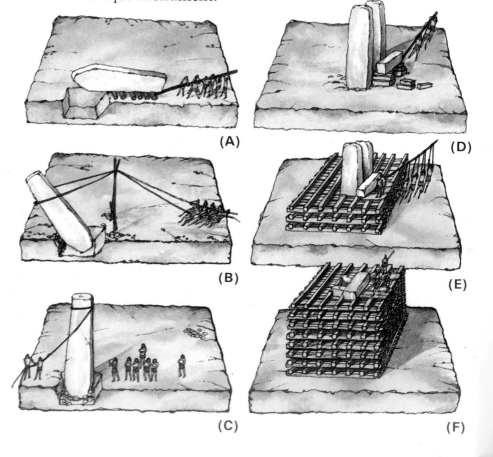

(A)

(B)

(C)

(D)

(E)

(F)

Above: A dagger carved into one of the stones at Stonehenge. On the same stone is a row of four axes, and there are similar carvings on other stones. Although visitors have carved their names on Stonehenge for centuries, these particular carvings were probably put there by those who used the temple.

What ceremonies were practiced at Stonehenge? It seems certain that rituals connected with the sun and moon took place there. Even as early as 2500 BC, the first enclosure and the Heel Stone were so aligned that they lay exactly along the line of the midsummer sunrise. There is also evidence that the users of Stonehenge at this time carefully observed the midwinter risings of the moon. At midsummer and midwinter, people from miles around may have gathered here for ceremonies which took place at the center of the monument or near the enclosing bank. A circle of over fifty pits appears to have been dug to hold offerings of water or other liquids, and then re-filled. Later, the cremated remains of people, possibly but not certainly sacrificial victims, were placed in some of these pits.

The changes which took place in the temple between 2000 and 1500 BC not only made it a much more impressive place, they placed greater emphasis on the midsummer sunrise and midwinter sunset. This may have been because the religious beliefs associated with the moon were going out of fashion. Furthermore, the sarsen circle and five trilithons now enclosed a very small area at the center of the temple. Whereas, earlier, many hundreds of people could watch and perhaps participate in all the rituals, now only twenty or thirty could. No doubt these were the chieftains and priests whose power partly depended on the mysteries of religion.

Outside the prehistoric village at Koumasa in southern Crete stood a cemetery of three circular stone tombs. These tombs, and other similar ones at nearby villages, contained many grave goods and ritual vessels, and sometimes clay models showing rituals. From these things, and other evidence, we can piece together the events at a Cretan funeral around 2200 BC.

The dead person has been brought to the cemetery and for the moment has been laid on the ground in front of the tomb. This tomb belongs to an extended family group of about 20 to 30 people. A few favorite personal belongings are placed on the stretcher with the body. They will be left in the tomb so that their dead owner will not come back to fetch them and haunt the village.

The immediate family gather around the body to drink a final "toast" to the deceased. They hold cups into which wine is poured from a special jug carried by the head of the family. When the toasting is over, the body and grave goods will be placed in the small square antechamber leading to the tomb. Then the men of the family will perform their ritual dance on the paved area in front of the tombs, linking arms and circling ever faster.

The rest of the village watches from beyond the wall which marks the edge of the sacred burial area.

Many days later, when the spirit is believed to have finally left the body, the corpse will be moved into the main circular chamber of the tomb. Here it will be laid alongside the remains of other members of the family stretching back over four or five centuries. A massive stone slab will then be placed across the entrance to the tomb. Its purpose will be as much to keep the dead in as the living out. Among these superstitious Cretan villagers, the dead ancestors are certainly venerated – but they are also feared.

Time Chart

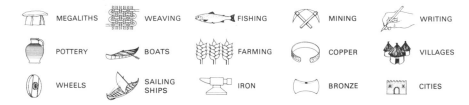

	MEGALITHS		WEAVING		FISHING		MINING		WRITING
	POTTERY		BOATS		FARMING		COPPER		VILLAGES
	WHEELS		SAILING SHIPS		IRON		BRONZE		CITIES

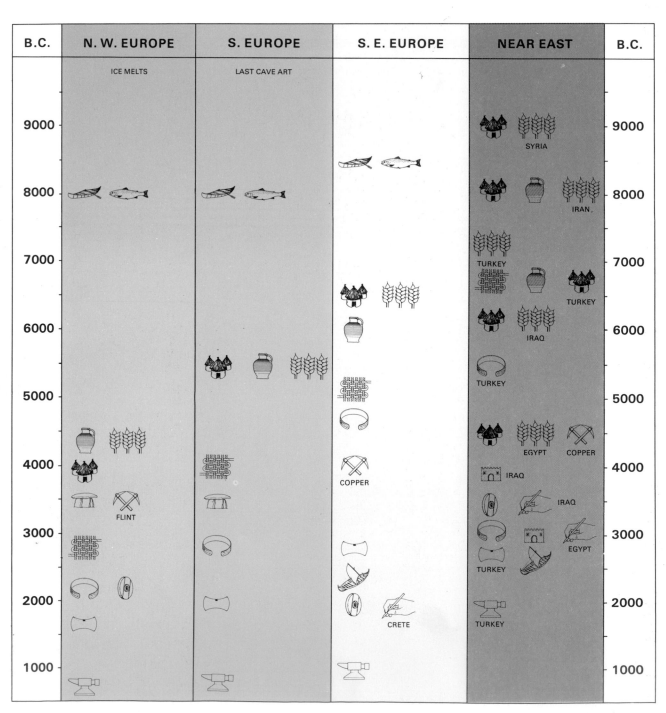

B.C.	N. W. EUROPE	S. EUROPE	S. E. EUROPE	NEAR EAST	B.C.
	ICE MELTS	LAST CAVE ART			
9000				SYRIA	9000
8000				IRAN	8000
7000				TURKEY	7000
				TURKEY	
6000				IRAQ	6000
5000				TURKEY	5000
4000	FLINT		COPPER	EGYPT COPPER / IRAQ / IRAQ	4000
3000				TURKEY / EGYPT	3000
2000			CRETE	TURKEY	2000
1000					1000

Index

Note: page numbers in *italics* refer to illustrations.